SPOTLIGHT ON NATURE
OWL

PAMELA DELL

CREATIVE EDUCATION · CREATIVE PAPERBACKS

Published by Creative Education and Creative Paperbacks
P.O. Box 227, Mankato, Minnesota 56002
Creative Education and Creative Paperbacks are imprints of The Creative Company
www.thecreativecompany.us

Design and production by Blue Design, Inc.
Art direction by Graham Morgan

Images by Dreamstime/Isselee, 1, Steve Allen, 21; Getty Images/Carlos Carreno, 17, Edmund Lowe Photography, 14, Gail Shotlander, 21, iavin photography, 4–5, Krzysztof Baranowski, 24, Scott Suriano, 18; Pexels/Anne-Marie Gionet-Lavoie, 27, mark broadhurst, 10, Pixabay, 9, Vincent M.A. Janssen, 12; Shutterstock/Le Do, 6, Oleksandr Lytvynenko, 6; Unsplash/Elisa Stone, 23, Zdeněk Macháček, cover; Wikimedia Commons/GT1976, 28, Luc Viatour, 11, Michael Gäbler, 29, Miscellaneous Items in High Demand, PPOC, Library of Congress, 8, 10, 14, 16, 20, 22, thibaudaronson, 29, U.S. Fish and Wildlife Service, 28, USFWS Mountain-Prairie, 16, W.carter, 2–3, 29, William Crochot, 15

Every effort has been made to contact copyright holders for material reproduced in this book. Any omissions will be rectified in subsequent printings if notice is given to the publisher.

Copyright © 2026 Creative Education, Creative Paperbacks
International copyright reserved in all countries. No part of this book may be reproduced in any form without written permission from the publisher.

Library of Congress Cataloging-in-Publication Data
Names: Dell, Pamela author
Title: Owl / by Pamela Dell.
Description: Mankato, Minnesota : Creative Education and Creative Paperbacks, [2026] | Series: Spotlight on nature | Includes bibliographical references and index. | Audience: Ages 10-13 | Audience: Grades 4-6 | Summary: "An immersive wildlife book for upper-elementary and middle-school readers, featuring a captivating owl family narrative, stunning photography, and educational tools like infographics, a glossary, and an index. Explores species, habitats, and conservation, making it perfect for nature lovers and young conservationists"— Provided by publisher.
Identifiers: LCCN 2025018182 (print) | LCCN 2025018183 (ebook) | ISBN 9798895810804 library binding | ISBN 9798896800330 paperback | ISBN 9798895812068 ebook
Subjects: LCSH: Owls—Juvenile literature
Classification: LCC QL696.S8 D456 2026 (print) | LCC QL696.S8 (ebook) | DDC 598.9/7—dc23/eng/20250707
LC record available at https://lccn.loc.gov/2025018182
LC ebook record available at https://lccn.loc.gov/2025018183

Printed in the United States

CONTENTS

MEET THE FAMILY	**4**
Great Horned Owls of North America	
LIFE BEGINS	**7**
FEATURED FAMILY	
Welcome to the World	8
First Meal	10
EARLY ADVENTURES	**13**
FEATURED FAMILY	
Getting the Hang of It	14
Give It a Try	16

LIFE LESSONS	**19**
FEATURED FAMILY	
This Is How It's Done	20
Practice Makes Perfect	22
ARE OWLS IN DANGER?	**25**
Family Album Snapshots	28
Words to Know	30
Learn More	31
Index	32

MEET THE FAMILY

Great Horned Owls of North America

The United States, Canada, Mexico, and Greenland make up the continent known as North America. This widespread territory includes numerous **ecosystems**, from prairies, plains, and woodlands to scorching deserts. It ranges from frozen arctic lands to tropical rainforests. The continent's wildlife includes approximately 457 mammal **species**, from giant polar bears to the teeny-tiny pygmy shrew. About 914 types of birds live here, as well as all kinds of reptiles, amphibians, insects, and plants. Among the many North American bird species is a group that has a legendary status in many cultures. This is the "wise old owl."

One of these, a great horned owl, **broods** in her tree-hollow nest. She laid two white eggs, and has kept them warm for five weeks. Now, one of them cracks open. A baby owl, or owlet, emerges. Two days later, the second egg hatches. For two little owlets, life begins.

CLOSE-UP
Vocalizing

Owlets begin making vocal sounds even before hatching. As adults, their vocalizing varies widely by species.

CHAPTER ONE
LIFE BEGINS

A spooky *who-whoooo* sound rises into the night air. Anyone listening might feel a little uneasy. But it's probably just an owl. Millions of these birds inhabit the world. About 250 different owl species make their homes on every continent except Antarctica. Owls live in forests and wide-open meadows. Some inhabit desert lands. Others are found only in cold arctic regions. Many owls find homes in tree holes or barn rafters. Some species burrow in the ground. But all of them are **raptors,** or birds of prey.

Owls have a striking appearance, thanks to their large eyes and intense stare. Most have squat rounded bodies, large heads, and short tails. Owls are divided into two families. Those known as barn owls have heart-shaped faces. Those in the other family, true owls, have round faces.

Owls are fierce, precise, and soundless hunters. Their diet depends on species. They may eat reptiles, fish, small rodents, or insects. Some eat scorpions and spiders. One large species, the great horned owl, has been

OWL MILESTONES

DAY (1)

- Weighs 1 to 1.2 ounces (34.7-37 gr)
- Entirely helpless, eyes unopened
- Nearly naked but with some downy white feathers
- Not yet able to control body temperature

known even to take down skunks. At the same time, few **predators** come after owls. Occasionally owls may end up the prey of another raptor. Given the opportunity, ground animals such as foxes or coyotes might also go after them. But owls are much more hunters than hunted.

Most owls are nocturnal or crepuscular. Nocturnal owls hunt at night. Crepuscular ones are active at dusk or dawn. The northern pygmy owl and the northern hawk owl are the only two species known to be diurnal, or daytime hunters.

An owl's size is also determined by its species. The world's smallest owl, the elf owl, grows to about 5 inches (12-14 centimeters) tall. The Blakiston's fish owl, the largest species, measures about 24 to 28 inches

CLOSE-UP
Brood patch
Before laying eggs, mother owls shed belly feathers to form a brood patch that keeps the eggs warm. Once the owlets grow, the feathers return.

― FEATURED ✦ FAMILY ―

Welcome to the World

The two little great horned owlets are not quite ready for the world. At only a few days old, their eyes are still sealed shut. Their bodies are covered with patchy, downy white feathers. They cannot even hold their heads up or regulate their own body temperature. The owlets weigh about 1.2 ounces (35 grams), and their bodies measure just 3 inches (7.6 centimeters) high. But their mother keeps them warm and safe underneath her or close beside her own body. She provides shelter even in the coldest of storms.

(60-72 cm) tall, and weighs 6.5 to 10.1 pounds (2.95-3.6 kilograms). And female owls are generally much bigger than males.

Some owl pairs mate for life. Others do not, but a male owl provides food for his mate while she broods. Once they've hatched, owlets must, first and foremost, stay alive. Their parents bring them food. But owl eggs usually hatch days apart. So the last hatched must even beware their older siblings—who might eat them if they get hungry enough.

8 DAYS
- Down replaced by grayish-white or yellowish-white immature feathers
- Flight feathers beginning to show in wings and tail

11 DAYS
- Eyes have opened

CLOSE-UP
Facial Disk

Owls' faces are encircled by a "wreath" of feathers called the facial disk. These feathers work like sound magnifiers. When hunting, the owl lifts them slightly to catch even the faintest sounds.

— FEATURED FAMILY —

First Meal

The hungry younger owlet is two days behind his sister in growth. She is bigger and stronger. Her taste for meat is now established. The owlets' parents must make sure sister doesn't eat brother. They do this by keeping the nest full of food. The mother owl's protective presence in the nest is important. So the owlets' father hunts for his children's dinner. He brings back prey to feed them all. In the nest, the mother owl tears the meat into small bits and feeds the begging owlets a late winter feast.

BARN OWLS are the only species that have heart-shaped faces.

② **WEEKS**
- About 50 percent of juvenile feathers have grown in
- Eyes begin to focus and work properly

③ **WEEKS**
- Primary feathers begin to show
- Ear tufts begin to grow in in small patches
- Begins pouncing on material in the nest to practice hunting

CLOSE-UP
Eyes
Owls' tube-shaped eyes let in lots of light, perfect for night hunting—but they can't move. Owls can only look straight ahead.

CHAPTER TWO
EARLY ADVENTURES

Owls are mostly loners. They spend little time together. A group of owls, called a parliament, may rest, or roost, with others of their species. But most roost alone. Owls roost after hunting, often choosing a roost near their nest. When they roost together, it may be to stay warm or to keep alert to any potential threat. Staying alert is especially important for owls that have owlets in the nest.

Younger **nestlings** may die of starvation if food gets scarce. Owlets that hatch first may eat their younger, weaker siblings. It's a dangerous time for these birds. Another danger comes from the owlets' attempts to remove waste from the nest. They learn to do this **instinctively**, but sometimes they fall out of the nest while trying to clean up. On the ground and still unable to fly, owlets make easy prey.

Yet owls grow up quickly. Most species purposely leave the nest after a few weeks. At first, they may perch only on nearby branches. During this

4 WEEKS
- Able to feed itself on food brought to nest
- Still sometimes fed by mother
- Flight feathers begin emerging

6 WEEKS
- Begins exercising wings and leaving nest
- Able to climb well
- May clamber on nearby branches, called branching

CLOSE-UP
Swivel Neck

Owls can turn their heads 270 degrees—so far right they end up looking left. This helps make up for eyes that can't move.

— FEATURED FAMILY —

Getting the Hang of It

Being stronger, the older great horned owlet takes most of the meat. But the owlet brother is hanging in all right. By mid-April, about three weeks old, the siblings' eyes are open and working well. Their down is being replaced by brownish-gray fluff and the beginnings of adult feathers. The owlets are lively in the nest now. They show defensive behaviors, especially when alarmed. They snap their bills. They hiss. They raise their wings then flap them downward. But these little guys are still totally dependent on their mother for food and protection.

time, owl siblings often stay close together as well as near the nest. At about a month old, many owl species are actively trying out their wings. They may take very short flights, and may not even be able to fly high enough to return to the nest. They continue to call out to their parents for food. But soon after **fledging**, owls begin to exercise their hunting skills. Young owls demonstrate apex predator abilities even before they are fully grown.

GREAT GREY OWL

(7) **WEEKS**
- Begins taking short, awkward test flights

(8) **WEEKS**
- Primary wing feathers mostly grown in
- Tail feathers still developing
- Fully mature

CLOSE-UP
Ear Tufts

Ear tufts are just feathers, not ears. They help owls communicate or stay hidden by making the head look less round.

 FEATURED FAMILY

Give It a Try

The great horned owlets are about six weeks old now. Their mother begins placing bits of meat on nearby branches to lure them out of the nest. Feeling brave and risky, the owlets snatch the food. They also begin exercising their wings, taking short, hop-like "flights." By mid-June, at 11 weeks old, the siblings are ready to take flight. As fledglings, their first flight is a bit sloppy, a quick trip from nest to ground. But little brother scrambles up a tree, beating his sister back into the nest.

OWLETS perch on branches near the nest.

(11) **WEEKS**
- Facial disk and white bib clearly visible

(12) **WEEKS**
- Adult breast feathers growing in
- Able to fly well

EARLY ADVENTURES 17

CLOSE-UP

Silent Flight

Owls fly nearly silently thanks to special flight feathers. The jagged leading edge and soft fringe on the trailing edge reduce air noise.

CHAPTER THREE
LIFE LESSONS

Owls are generally long-lived birds. But their average lifespan varies widely according to species. Typically, the larger the species the longer the lifespan. Those in captivity usually live much longer than wild owls because they face fewer dangers. In the wild, tiny elf owls might live three to six years. In captivity, they can live up to ten years. The large Eurasian eagle owl lives about 20 years or up to 60 years in captivity.

Owls are fiercely territorial. They need large stretches of connected territory to find enough prey and to search for mates. They are also silent, secretive creatures. So when an owl calls out, those sounds usually have a purpose. It may be to alert others that the territory is already taken or to communicate with a potential mate.

Young owls are clumsy and awkward as they learn to fly and hunt. But as they mature, they become confident predators. By the fall the owlets

(4) **MONTHS**

▸ Adult back feathers growing in

(5) **MONTHS**

▸ Adult head feathers fully grown in

are full-grown and ready to mate themselves, though owls usually mate early in the year.

After an elaborate mating ritual, a pair of owls works together to raise their young. Many species stay together for life, breeding year after year. Other species raise a single brood together, then part and find other mates the following years.

Owls are also not nest builders. They search out some convenient spot and lay their eggs there. Mostly, this means taking over a nest left empty by some other animal. It might be a crow, a hawk, or some other bird. Some owl species claim the nests or burrows of foxes or other mammals. Tree-dwelling species look for natural holes in a tree trunk, called cavities or hollows. At most, owls may add a little material to

─── FEATURED FAMILY ───

This Is How It's Done

Flying was dangerous at first. Until he got the hang of it, the young great horned owl had a few close calls. Time on the ground meant some bigger animal might make a meal of him. More than once he had to stand straight up and perfectly still against a tree trunk to avoid being seen. But now it's September. The owlet is no longer an owlet. To prove it, he flies silently above a grassy field. The first bunny gets away. But the next one is an easier catch.

6 MONTHS	1 YEAR
▸ Fully feathered	▸ Able to begin breeding

the nest they occupy, such as animal fur or a layer of downy feathers for warmth and softness.

A pair of owls will often return to the same nest every year. In years when little food is available, owls may not even mate. But after only a few months of life, owls "know the ropes" and the lay of the land. These young, powerful raptors are now ready for the world. If they are lucky, they can expect a long, productive life.

CLOSE-UP
Ears

Owl ears are simply holes in the sides of their heads. But in many species, the ears do not line up. The right is usually set higher. This uneven positioning allows for pinpoint accuracy in locating sounds even when it's too dark to see prey.

--- FEATURED FAMILY ---

Practice Makes Perfect

One late October night, the young great horned owl perches high in a pine tree. He is full-sized now, with ear tufts and adult feathers. Being a skilled hunter, he's stopped begging for food. Chilly fall breezes rustle in the shadowy trees. The owl hears every sound. Something skitters through the dry leaves below. The young predator swoops down swiftly, noiselessly. In seconds he has caught a fat, unwitting squirrel. After his meal, it is finally time. The owl sails into the darkness. Time to find his own territory away from home.

Owls aren't builders. They find tree cavities or other **convenient** spots for their future brood.

(2) YEARS — Sexually mature

13-20 YEARS — End of life

LIFE LESSONS 23

CHAPTER FOUR
ARE OWLS IN DANGER?

Looking at the big picture, it's easy to say owls are safe as a group of species. Globally, they number in the millions. They are even highly respected and honored in many cultures. But owls do face dangers in the modern world. The worst of these is loss of habitats due to human activities.

Owls lose their prey when they lose their land. Destroying old buildings and dead or dying trees harms owls like barn owls that nest there. Clearing land for farming or building also takes away their homes. Pesticides add another danger. When people use poisons to kill rodents or other prey, the poisons enter the owls' bodies. Also, many owls fly low to hunt. They may be hurt or killed by hitting power lines or colliding with cars. In the U.S., it is illegal to hunt owls. But this is not true everywhere. And some species, like the great horned owl, are illegally hunted.

Since owls like to hide away and many hunt at night, some species are difficult to count accurately. But the International Union for Conservation of Nature (IUCN) Red List includes a number of **endangered** species. The

CLOSE-UP
Talons
All raptors have toes ending in sharp claws, called talons. An owl's foot has four powerful talons.

Congo Bay owl and the forest owlet, found in India, are only two of these.

Various worldwide organizations are dedicated to protecting owls and their habitats. Studies on owl health and habitat loss are part of these efforts. Two very active U.S. organizations are the Nature Conservancy and the Owl Research Institute. These work around the globe, often with partners. Some of their projects include preserving habitats and tracking owl activity by putting harmless tags on them. The public is welcome to contribute. Two ways people can join in are by donating or volunteering. Citizens can also contact elected officials and attend events in support of owl conservation efforts. One way to help closer to home is by using rodent traps instead of poison. Another is to think twice before tearing down a tree or a building that might house owls and their owlets. When anyone hears a who-whoooo in the night, that's a reminder of how important it is that owls keep on having a voice.

FAMILY ALBUM
SNAPSHOTS

A **barred owl's** call sounds something like Who cooks for you? Who cooks for you all? Some say its call sounds like a neighing horse.

If necessary, **burrowing owls** will dig their own nest homes. But they prefer taking over the underground burrows of small animals like prairie dogs.

The **Sula barn owl** of Indonesia is so hard to sight that only one specimen has ever been caught, that in 1938.

Snowy owls are one of the world's heaviest owls. This weight comes from the thick feathers that cover their bodies, legs, and feet to help them stay warm.

The **little owl** spends some of its time in daylight hours and will bravely perch openly even where lots of human activity is going on.

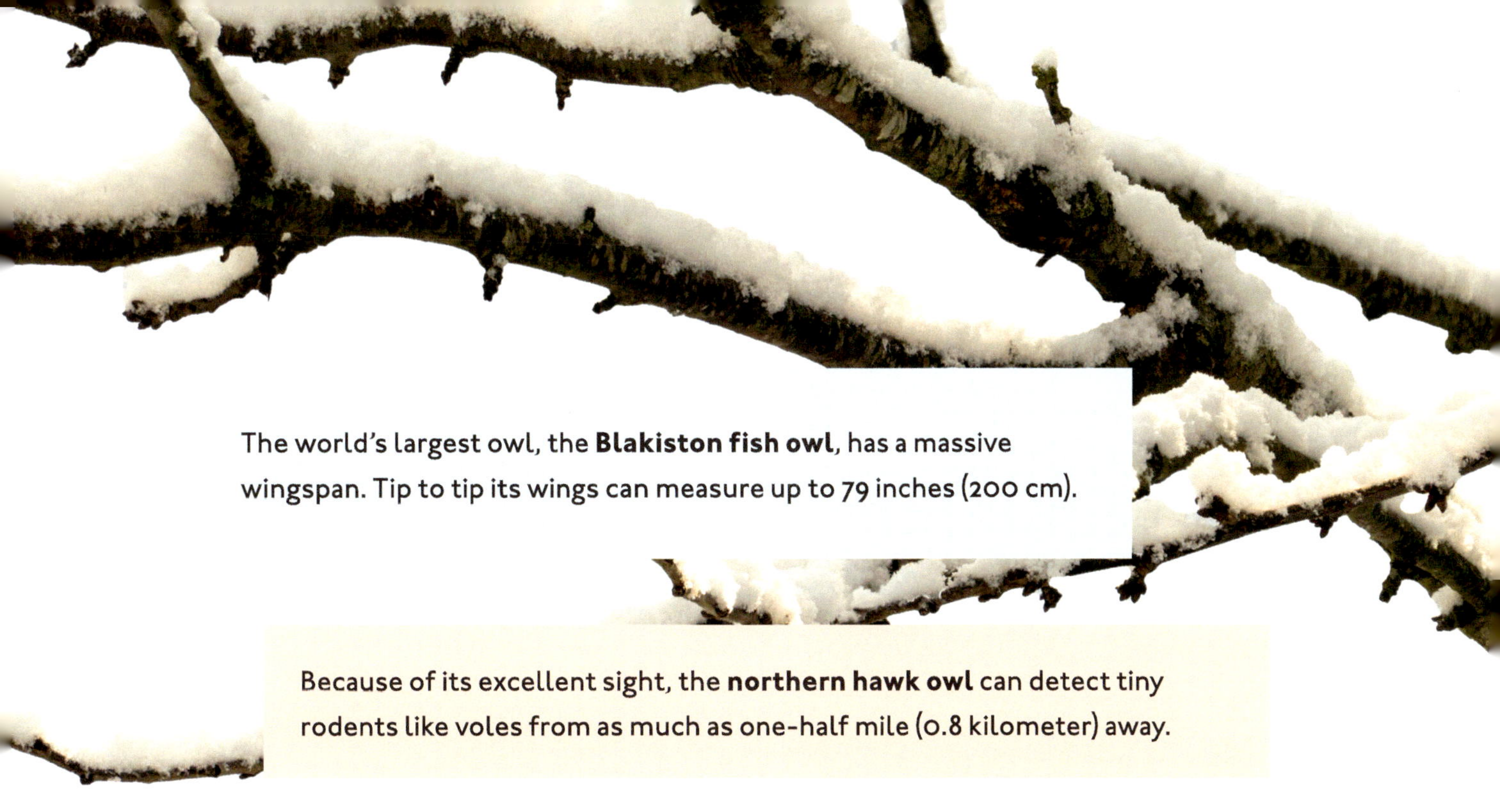

The world's largest owl, the **Blakiston fish owl**, has a massive wingspan. Tip to tip its wings can measure up to 79 inches (200 cm).

Because of its excellent sight, the **northern hawk owl** can detect tiny rodents like voles from as much as one-half mile (0.8 kilometer) away.

Elf owls, found in the deserts of Mexico and the southwestern U.S., are about the size of a sparrow. They weigh no more than a golf ball. .

Long-whiskered owlets, native to northern Peru, are relatives of the elf owl. They have fan-like whiskers and no ear tufts.

Great horned owls are sometimes called tigers of the sky because of their excellent hunting skills and ability to take down large prey.

Barn owls, nicknamed straw owls, church owls, and ghost owls, tend to nest near human dwellings. They are known for their spine-tingling nighttime shrieks.

WORDS to Know

brood — the job of mother birds (or sometimes the father) to sit on nest eggs to keep them warm until they hatch; a group of owlets or other baby birds

ecosystem — a community of plants and animals that live together in a specific place along with nonliving things, like rocks, dirt, and water

endangered — at risk of dying out completely

fledge — having wing feathers large enough for flight

fledgling — a bird newly able to fly

instinctive — having an inborn or naturally occurring knowledge or understanding

nestling — a newly hatched bird, too young to leave the nest

predator — an animal that hunts other animals

raptor — a bird of prey, with curved sharp beak, or bill, and sharp claws, or talons

species — a group of living things that have shared characteristics and are able to reproduce with one another

LEARN MORE

Books

Bodden, Valerie. *Owls (Amazing Animals series)*. Minneapolis, MN: Creative Paperbacks, 2022.

van Frankenhuyzen, Robbyn Smith. *Adopted by an Owl: The True Story of Jackson the Owl*. Ann Arbor, MI: Sleeping Bear Press, 2016.

Whipple, Annette. *Whooo Knew: The Truth About Owls*. New Rochelle, NY: Reycraft Books, 2021.

Wilson, Mark. *Owling: Enter the World of the Mysterious Birds of the Night*. Pownal, VT: Storey Publishing, LLC, 2019.

Websites

"Superb Owls." National Geographic Kids. https://kids.nationalgeographic.com/animals/birds/article/superb-owls

"Owl." Britannica Kids. https://kids.britannica.com/kids/article/owl/353584.

"13 Fun Facts About Owls." National Audubon Society. https://www.audubon.org/news/13-fun-facts-about-owls

Documentaries

Gowac, Joe, director/photographer. "*The Fledgling 4: A Wildlife Documentary.*" Available on YouTube, 2024.

Nadaskay, Istvan, director. "*Owl's Odyssey.*" 2013. Available on Prime Video.

Rover, Jorn [head of Doculights]. "*Owls: Masters of the Night.*" Doculights, 2020. Available on Prime Video.

Note: Every effort has been made to ensure that any websites listed above were active at the time of publication. However, because of the nature of the Internet, it is impossible to guarantee that these sites will remain active indefinitely or that their contents will not be altered.

Visit

LAKE ERIE NATURE AND SCIENCE CENTER
Join the Center's annual evening "Owl Prowl" to have close encounters with many owl species, plus join the owl scavenger hunt.
28728 Wolf Road
Bay Village, OH 44140

NATIONAL AVIARY
Learn about many species, and make a personal connection with a real live owl as it perches on your gloved hand.
770 Arch St.
Pittsburgh, PA 15212

INTERNATIONAL FESTIVAL OF OWLS
Visit this event, held annually in early March. It's an opportunity to learn more about owls and join many fun family activities, such as building a nest box for an owl.
Events throughout the town
Houston, MN 55943

WEST COAST FALCONRY
Sign up for the Falconry's Owl Encounter with live owls, or take a night-time trek to hear owl stories and legends and maybe spot a few owls on the wing.
10308 Spring Valley Rd
Marysville, CA 95901

INDEX

Barn owl, 7, 11, 25, 28, 29
brood patch, 8
conservation, 25, 26
ear tufts, 11, 16, 22, 29
eyes, 7, 8, 9, 11, 12, 14
facial disk, 10, 17
Great horned owl, 4, 7, 8, 14, 16, 20, 22, 25, 29
habitat loss, 26
lifespan, 19

mating, 9, 20, 22
nocturnal, 8
owlet, 4, 6, 8, 9, 10, 13, 14, 16, 17, 19, 20, 26, 29
predators, 8, 15, 19, 22
silent flight, 18
swivel neck, 14
talons, 21
territory, 4, 19, 22
vocalizations, 6